Karol Krčmár

KIRIGAMI

THE PAPER KINGDOM

The Art of Paper Cutting and Folding

McCabe Children's Press

© 2005 by Karol Krčmár
© 2005 by ToolSquare
© 2005 by Kotzig Publishing

ISBN 0-9715411-6-7

About the Author

Slovak designer Karol Krčmár
is a member of the following organizations:
SUFA – Slovak Union of Fine Arts,
Union of Industrial Designers of Slovakia,
IAPMA – International Association
of Hand Papermakers and Paper Artists,
UNIMA – Union Internationale de la Marionnette.

He won the Gold Medal at the World Fair of Inventions
and New Products INPEX XII in Pittsburgh, PA, USA, in 1996
for his designs of wooden kinetic toys called Carlo,
which brought him international acclaim.
The World Organization for the Protection of Children
Rights UNICEF, Geneva, has accepted these toys into
its sales program.

For his graphic designs, Karol Krčmár
won the prestigious Andy Warhol Prize,
awarded by the Museum of Andy Warhol
and Andy Warhol Society in Medzilaborce,
Slovakia.

KIRIGAMI, the Paper Kingdom
is his first book and has already sold thousands
of copies in the Czech Republic, Slovakia,
Hungary and Germany.

The Author lives with his wife Lujza
and their two children, Katarina and Matej,
in Bratislava, the capital city of the Slovak Republic
in Central Europe.

For more information about the author, please visit
www.kotzigpublishing.com/krcmar

My dear kids and dear friends,

Can you cut sheets of paper? If the answer is yes, then this book is designed just for you. All complicated things are composed of smaller, easier ones. So, as well, you will discover that the masks, cut toys and three dimensional pictures shown in this book come into being step by step, cut by cut.

When you have made the decision to follow these steps with me, your hands will make the Paper Kingdom grow before your eyes. As your tables and bookshelves begin to fill with your projects, your skill and excitement will grow. Share your enthusiasm and send a home-made toy to a friend or relative.

To begin the fun you will only need a piece of paper and a good pair of scissors.

Karol Kúmar

Table of Contents

THE KING'S ROYAL COURT

BOGEYMEN AND OTHER CREATURES

From Ancient Egypt

Creatures from Outer Space

PRINCESS' TOYS AND NETS FOR DRAGON

GREETING CARDS

On the tail end

Tools and Materials

Paper

Office paper, white or colored, is the most suitable for projects in this book. In some cases, poster board or artist's paper would be better, even though this kind of paper can be harder to cut once folded. Your parents or other adults can help you with this.

Size of Paper

Do you know what a size **A4** paper is? It is similar to letter size and we will be using it the most. When you divide that size sheet of paper in half along the shorter side, you get the smaller paper, size **A5** (half letter). Paper size **A3** is twice as large as size A4 and similar to 11" x 17" paper.

half letter (A5)   letter (A4)   11" x 17" (A3)

Scissors

Choose scissors that work best for you. Children should use rounded end scissors. If sharply pointed scissors are used, an adult should supervise. In some cases, small manicure scissors can be used.

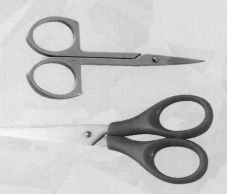

Terms and Symbols

You are starting off on an exciting journey, cutting your way from a two-dimensional world of flat surfaces into a three dimensional world where you can add width, height and depth. On every page, signs are erected that help you happily reach the end. You'll also find some signs on your road to the Paper Kingdom. Now it's time to show you what they mean.

A dashed line shows where the sheet of paper should be folded. If you fold and squeeze along it, a sharp fold will result.

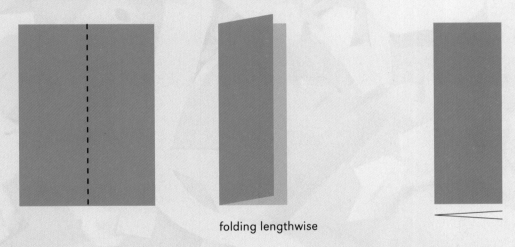

folding lengthwise

A sharp V means the paper has already been folded in half. The fold is at the tip of the V-sign.

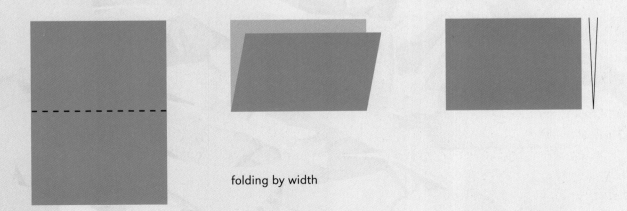

folding by width

A solid line means **a cut**. Sometimes little scissors placed at the begining of the line will remind you.

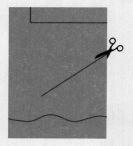 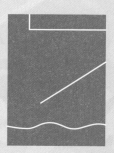

A dotted line means **a score**. The best way to do this: hold the ruler tightly against the line where you want to fold the sheet of paper and run the tip of your scissors close to edge of ruler. Press the tip of the scissors to the paper lightly. If needed, apply this score to both sides of paper.

 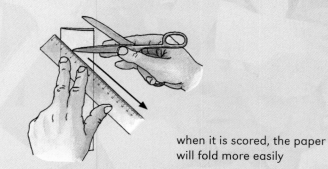

when it is scored, the paper will fold more easily

An arched line means **curling**. This means that you make the entire sheet of paper, or a part of it, rounded. The whole paper can be curled in this way: grasp the edges and pull it over the edge of a table. A paper strip can be pulled over the edge of a scissors while pressed by the thumb (as if making curly ribbons for a gift package).

When you see **a hand**, unfold slightly and push the paper inside. Next carefully pull from the inside until you reach the end of the cuts and squeeze along the folds.

Bending means the folded paper should be slightly opened and bent in on the fold: in this way its direction will be changed. After this modification, the inside of the paper will be on the outside and the outer sides will face in.

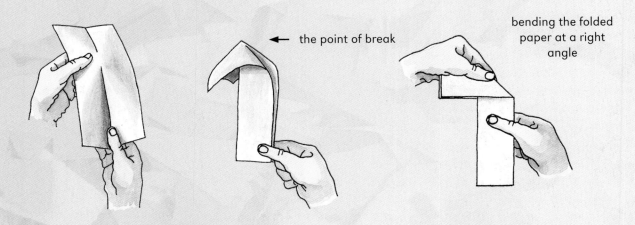

← the point of break

bending the folded paper at a right angle

Simple Caps

At the beginning, we can try
something really simple.
With one, or just a few cuts, you can
make many different caps.

Helmet or Flat Cap

1. Fold a sheet of size A4 paper in half. Hold it so that the fold points to you.

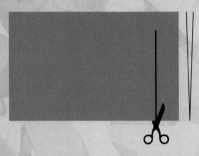

2. On the right side of the folded piece of paper make a perpendicular cut of about 1" (3 cm) from the edge. End it 1" (3 cm) from the opposite edge.

3. Hold the piece of paper with the fold at the top. Open it and push the strip made by the cut down and in.

4. A gap is created and you can put this simple flat cap on your head, with the small strip in the back.

15

Little Red Cap

If you have managed the flat cap, with just one more cut a little cap will be created suitable for a character from a well-known Slovak fairy tale.

1. Into the fold of a folded piece of size A4 paper...

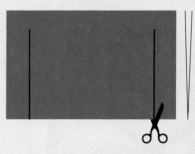

2. ... make two straight perpendicular cuts (on either side) at a distance of 1" (3 cm) from the edge. End the cuts 1" (3 cm) from the opposite edge.

3. Open slightly and put the cut piece of paper on the head; pull the side strips down...

4. ... and place them under the ears.

Tip:
When you make this cap from a white piece of paper it will protect a baby from glaring sunshine. If he or she pulls it off, you can easily make a new one!

Cap of Skillfulness

Why such an unusual name as Cap of Skillfulness? Well, it is called this because whoever cuts out and places this on their head will be protected from the Lady Unskillful who is always around wherever something is being made. How can you make this cap? Some more cuts will need to be made.

1. Fold a piece of size A4 paper in half.

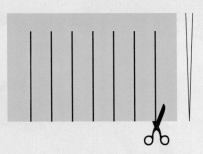

2. Starting at the fold, make as many cuts as you can approximately 1" (3 cm) apart. It should look like a wide comb.

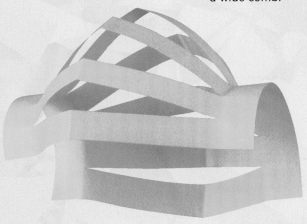

3. Open the piece of paper, spread it gently and, holding it by the shorter sides, place it on your head.

The Paper Kingdom

Do you think I only make things up and that the Paper Kingdom doesn't exist? But it does! I have been there. King Notebook I has sent for me because a disaster has happened. While Princess Notepad was watching the frightful Dragon named Shredder fly over the castle, she fell into a deep paper chasm. As the world's greatest Paperologist, I was called to help them pull her out. How did I get there? By helicopter of course!

Helicopter

1. Cut off a 1" (3 cm) strip from a sheet of size A5 paper. Make cuts from both sides halfway down the length; cut into the width about one-third on each side. Score on the dotted lines. Cut down the middle from the top to approximately ½" (1 cm) of the side cuts.

2. Fold the bottom pieces on top of each other, then twist the ends so they will not separate. Slightly bend the strips in opposite directions to separate. Drop it and watch your helicopter rotate and fly.

In the Paper Kingdom, at Origami Airport, His Majesty King Notebook I and his entire Court have been waiting for me. We rushed at once to the Paper Chasm. Our problem was the longest piece of paper in the whole Kingdom wasn't long enough to reach the bottom. But how to make it longer? It is not without reason that I am known as the world's best Paperologist. I always think of something! This time, I have thought of a ladder.

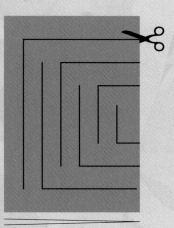

1. Following the picture, fold a piece of size A4 paper in half and make an L-shaped cut starting at the fold and about 1" (2 cm) in from both edges. End the cut about 1" (2 cm) from the opposite edge. Make a similar cut from the other side of the fold but slightly smaller. Continue in this way, making each cut from the opposite side and slightly smaller than the one before until you have at least four cuts. More cuts will make a longer ladder.

Ladder

3. Take the center and pull it up to form a ladder.

2. Open the cut and half folded piece of paper carefully. Flatten out the fold with the palm of your hand.

However, this ladder hasn't reached Princess Notepad at the bottom of the chasm. It will be necessary to think up something else.

Rope

1. Take a rectangular piece of paper and cut a strip to within 1" (2 cm) of the opposite edge. Starting at the opposite side of the paper, near the first cut, make another cut to within 1" (2 cm) of the opposite edge. Continue in this way, from one side to the other, until you have a really long strip of paper.

Spiral

1. Take a piece of paper, and starting close to the edge, cut out a circle. Continue cutting a long curved cut parallel to the outer edge of the circle until you reach the middle.

It seemed Princess Notepad was going to be saved, but as soon as she caught the end of the rope and we started to pull her up, the rope broke! Then I remembered how the Native Americans made long straps for binding sticks to use for their Teepees. They cut a circle from a piece of leather and then cut it into a spiral.

By my command, and King Notebook I's order, each inhabitant of the Paper Kingdom cut one very long spiral strip. We braided them together to make a thick rope and, with this, pulled Princess Notepad to safety.

Stretcher

1. Fold a rectangular piece of paper lengthwise. With the edge of the fold facing you, make a straight perpendicular cut about 1" (2 cm) in from the side. End it about 1" (2 cm) from the opposite side. Make a second cut of the same size from the other side. Make a third cut of the same size starting from the fold. At the opposite side of the folded paper, make the exact same cuts as on the first side. Unfold carefully to make the stretcher as pictured below.

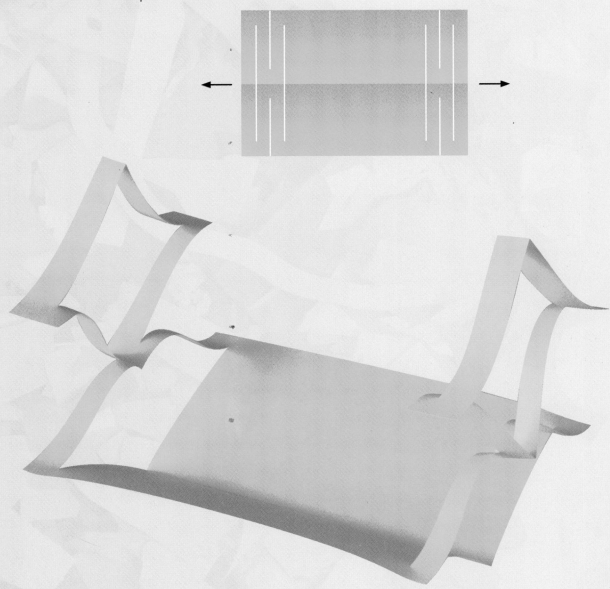

What happiness!! As a reward, King Notebook I gave me 1,999 absolutely blank sheets of art paper for drawings. He praised me and gave me a royal title, World's Greatest Paperologist. He wanted to give me Princess Notepad as my wife, but I was already married. Princess Notepad was pleased because she loved Prince Calendar. He always remembered birthdays, anniversaries and holidays.

A banquet followed with the finest delicacies. There were paper rolls filled with whipped cellulose. Boxes of packing peanuts were decorated with doilies. Everybody drank genuine, non-adulterated Ink, Vintage '99. Exhausted by the rescue, ceremonies and banquet, I breathed a sigh of relief and looked at my surroundings. I was standing on the balcony of a beautiful castle and on the slope under it were the red roofs of cute little houses surrounded by lovely green trees. Let's cut out this beautiful Countryside…

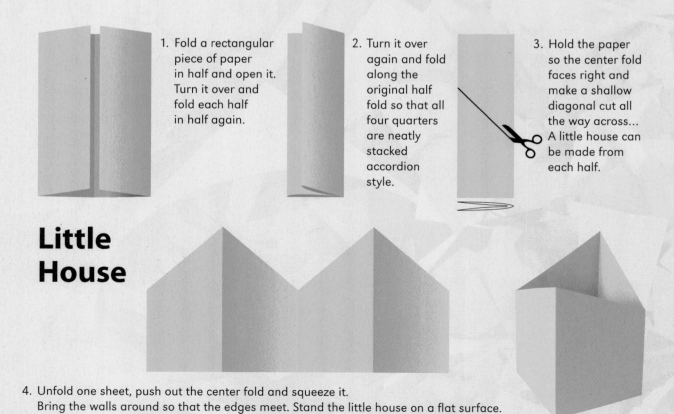

1. Fold a rectangular piece of paper in half and open it. Turn it over and fold each half in half again.

2. Turn it over again and fold along the original half fold so that all four quarters are neatly stacked accordion style.

3. Hold the paper so the center fold faces right and make a shallow diagonal cut all the way across… A little house can be made from each half.

Little House

4. Unfold one sheet, push out the center fold and squeeze it. Bring the walls around so that the edges meet. Stand the little house on a flat surface.

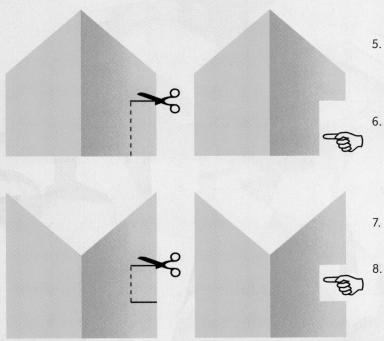

Door

5. Hold the paper so that the center fold faces left. Make a perpendicular cut about halfway up into one of the shorter folds. The cut should be to the center of that fold. Score along the dotted line.
6. Open the sheet slightly and push the door inside. Pull from the inside to the ends of the cut and fold the cut back on itself to crease it.

Window

7. Hold the center fold to the right and make two identical, parallel cuts into the center fold only. Score along the dotted line.
8. Push the paper inside, between the cuts, by slightly opening the walls of the little house. Pull the paper from the inside to the ends of the cuts and fold the cut back on itself to crease it. After unfolding, the little window should look like the one seen in the fold in the illustration below.

Roof

9. The roof is the top of the house. It can easily be made from a rectangular sheet of red paper, folded in half and placed on top of the little house.

Castle

Foundations

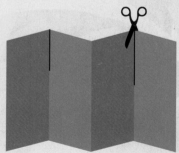

1. In the beginning you can make a small castle from a sheet of size A4 paper. Fold it half and then fold each half back on itself. Now you have quarter-folds. It should look like an accordion.

2. With the original (middle) fold pointing at you, cut into the left outside fold about one-third. Cut into the right outside fold slightly more, but less than one-half.

3. Cut two strips of paper from the top of each of the outer sides, the left one small and the right one bigger, just like in the picture.

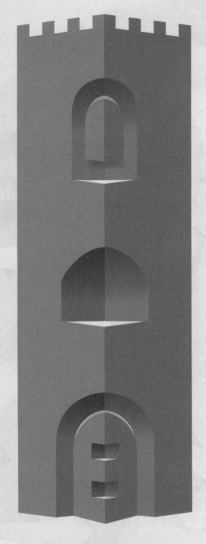

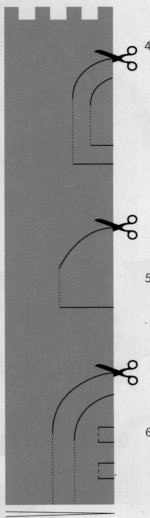

Double Window

4. Make two arched cuts in the middle fold, one bigger and one smaller underneath it (see illustration). Add two straight, perpendicular cuts below. Score along the dotted lines. Create a double window: start by pushing the window inside and squeezing the fold. Next push the small one in the opposite direction and squeeze the fold.

Half-window

5. Cut it out in the same fashion as the straight window in the Little House (previous project) except the upper cut will have an arched shape.

Gate

6. Make two arched cuts, one bigger and one smaller underneath it (see illustration). Under these cuts, make two pairs of very short cuts perpendicular to the fold.

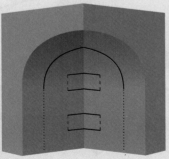

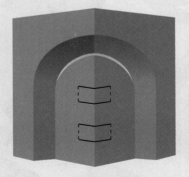

7. Score along the dotted lines from the end of the arched cuts, parallel to the fold

8. In this way you've created two gates: one large and one small. Push the large gate inward, squeeze the fold and then push the little one out in the opposite direction and squeeze the fold.

9. Lastly, push the little windows in the gate inside.

Battlement

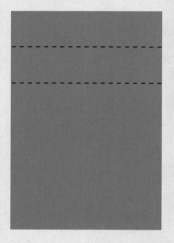

10. In the upper part of the left side of the foundation make two parallel, sharp...

11. ...accordion folds.

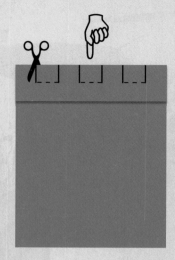

12. Make six cuts into the top going almost to the edge of the fold. Gently open the folds and fold back and down between every other cut to make them flat. Now you have created the battlement of the castle.

The Battlements are formed by an elevated wall in which there are gaps. The gaps enabled shooting and allowed the defenders to hide behind the elevated parts.

Balcony

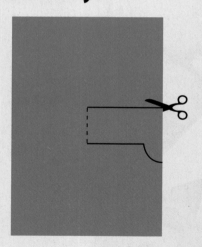

13. From the back of the left fold, start two cuts approximately in the middle of the paper. The top cut will be perpendicular to the fold and the bottom will start with a curved quarter arch and then become parallel to the top cut. Both cuts must end at the same point. Score along the dotted line.

Rounded corner

14. Make a bent corner into the left wall of the Castle. Begin with a small arched cut starting just under the battlement and going down slightly. Score along the dotted line and then fold it back. Make a little window in the fold (see picture of the castle).

Battlement brackets

15. In the bottom fold, push every other piece between the cuts forward. Push them out to the end of the cuts and squeeze the folds. These are the brackets which support the protruding battlement.

Roof

16. Bend the top of the right side of the castle foundation forward to the end of the cut and then fold it forward once again. Open the second fold slightly to form the roof.

Guard Turret

17. From the back of the right fold and beginning just under the level of the roof, make a diagonal cut downwards. Score along the dotted line. Make two windows; the top will have a diagonal cut and then a straight cut. They must end at the same distance. Score along the dotted line. The second window can be two straight cuts. When you open the fold slightly, push the guard turret out and the windows in.

Tip:
Your castle needn't be the same as in the Paper Kingdom. Maybe you would like more windows or balconies, or more plentiful battlements; it is your castle so make whatever you wish. You can also make it bigger by starting with a size A3 paper or even bigger made from a larger size of poster board. But I would practice first on smaller paper.

A lot of trees grew in the Paper Kingdom. Around the Castle there were tall spruces and fruit trees in small gardens next to the little houses.

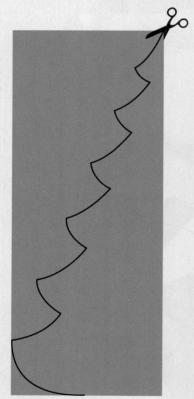

Spruce Tree

Spruce branches are smaller towards the top of the tree so that their lower branches can also receive sunlight.

1. Fold a sheet of paper in half. The fold will be the trunk of the tree. Start cutting downwards from the tip of the fold and make each branch slightly larger until you reach the bottom of the tree. Cut each branch with one curved cut going out and a smaller curved cut coming back in.

2. The spruces can be small and wide or thin and high. It depends on the size of paper you choose and whether you fold it through the width or length.

The more trees you cut the more lush your Paper Kingdom will be.

1. Starting at the fold, cut a half silhouette of a broad-leafed tree into a folded sheet of paper. Make a treetop by using curved cuts and then make the trunk with a vertical cut below. Cut a little hill with a large curved cut from the trunk to the edge of the paper. This will also be the base to make your tree stand upright.

2. On the treetop, parallel to the main fold...

3. ...make several folds like an accordion. Next you can cut out pears from the front or from behind.

Pear Tree

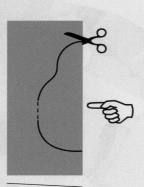

4. As shown in the picture, cut out a pear with two curved cuts. Score along the dotted line. Push the paper between the cuts inside to the other side and squeeze the fold

5. If you cut more pears, be careful you don't cut into others. You can avoid this if you cut pears of different sizes.

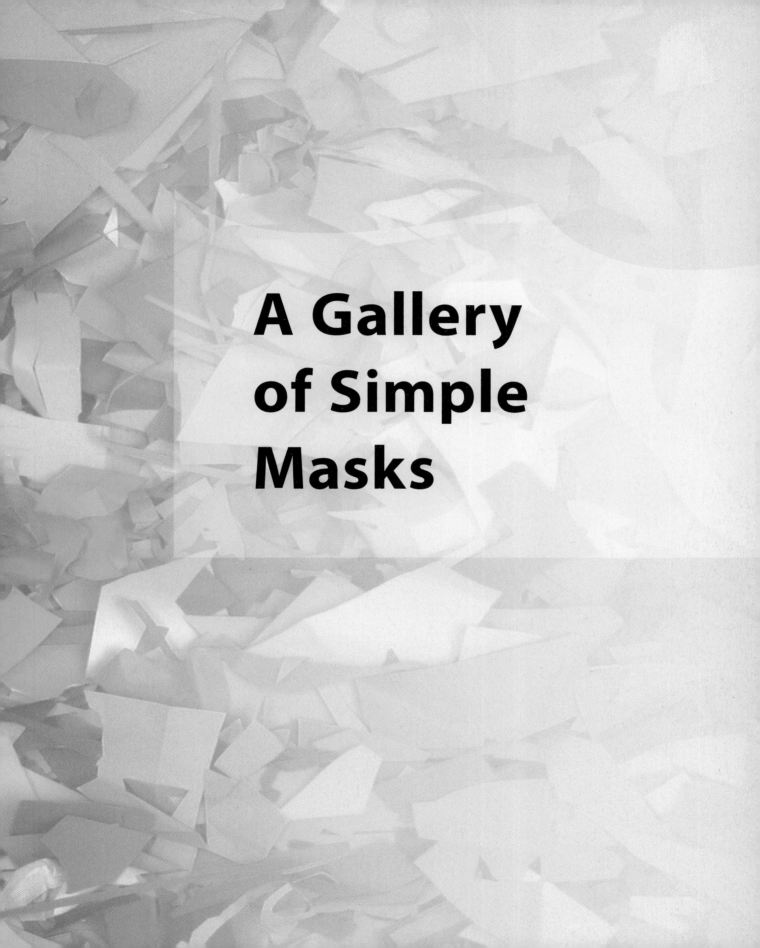

A Gallery of Simple Masks

Now, back to the banquet being given to celebrate the freedom of Princess Notepad. Carnival is at its climax. It was surprising to find everyone with spiky Jester's hats, although each was of a different color. I asked if they had other hats or masks and the answer was "no." So, I thought some up and taught the people how to make them. You can cut some also. If you don't have a piece of paper of the same color as the picture, don't worry. Use what you have, it's all about having fun.

The Basic Mask

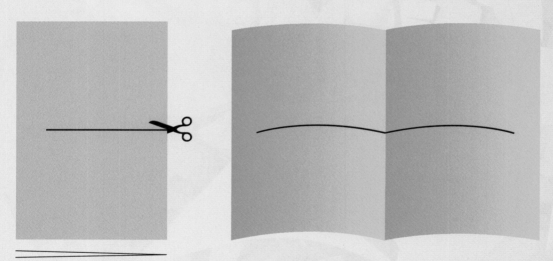

1. The basic mask will be a piece of paper folded in half. At the halfway point along the fold, make a vertical cut almost to the end of the paper. We will call this the main cut.

2. Open the paper so that the fold is vertical and the cut divides it into two horizontal parts.

   Tip:
   Size A4 paper will be right for smaller children. Older kids might want to use a larger size.

Tip:
The main cut should be one-forth the circumference of your head. Measure your head with a string and then fold the string in half, and then in half again. This is how long the cut should be.

3. Gently pull each side of the cut
   in the opposite direction. The opening
   for your head is now created. After putting
   the mask on your head, the upper part will be somewhat like a headband
   and the lower part will fit around the back of your head. To make it easier
   to place on your head, make vertical folds on the lower part from the ends
   of the cuts to the edges of the paper.

You can give these two parts different shapes. You must realize however, that any cuts you make into the folded sheet of paper will be duplicated once opened. That means, for example, if you wish to have a mask of an animal with two ears, you should cut a half-head with one ear. If you want a circle, you should cut a semi-circle into the folded paper. You can try this on the next mask, which will be the Sun.

Sun

1. Fold a piece of paper in half and cut a semi-circle starting at the upper end of the fold and going to the lower end. Open it and check if the circle is a success.

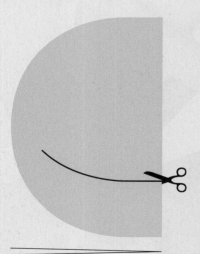

2. Fold the circle and make the main cut in the shape of a little half smile, curving upwards, in the lower part of the fold. After opening, this cut should look like a smile.

3. Push the lower part back and place the mask on your head.

Wind

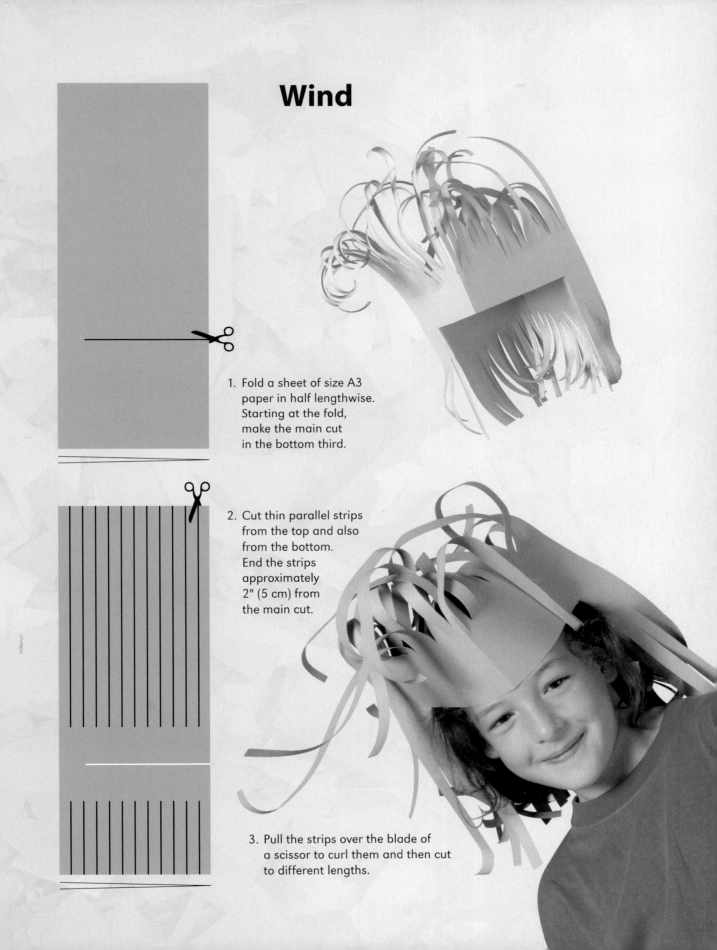

1. Fold a sheet of size A3 paper in half lengthwise. Starting at the fold, make the main cut in the bottom third.

2. Cut thin parallel strips from the top and also from the bottom. End the strips approximately 2" (5 cm) from the main cut.

3. Pull the strips over the blade of a scissor to curl them and then cut to different lengths.

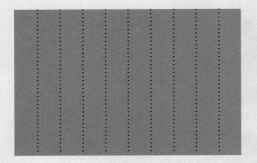

1. Take a sheet of size A3 paper and...

2. ...accordion fold it so you have many folds.

Rain

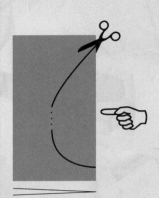

3. Cut raindrops into the folds with two cuts each. The lower cut is a quarter cut curving upwards. The second, upper cut is slanted down towards the curved bottom cut. The ends of the cuts should be the same distance from the fold. Score along the dotted line for each raindrop.

4. You can cut raindrops from both sides of the folded sheet, but as was explained with the Pear Tree, the cuts must not cross over each other. Help yourself by making a row of raindrops of one size and then cut the new row of raindrops a bit lower. Push each raindrop in the opposite direction and squeeze the folds.

Cloud

2. Holding the fold vertically, make a curved main cut following the shape of the lower edge of the cloud. The cut should be in the bottom third of the cloud. Remember to size it for your head.

1. Cut a half cloud shape into a folded sheet of size A3 paper. Start at the top right of the fold and finish it at the lower right end.

3. Hold the upper part in one hand, push the lower part back, and you can put the mask on your head.

Apple

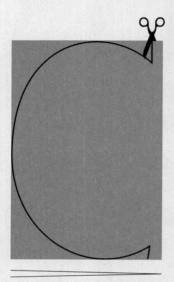

1. Starting at the fold, cut a half apple into a folded sheet of size A4 paper. The upper part will be a short stem.

3. Open the mask and put it on your head.

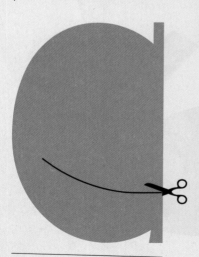

2. Following the picture, make a main cut into the bottom part of the apple.

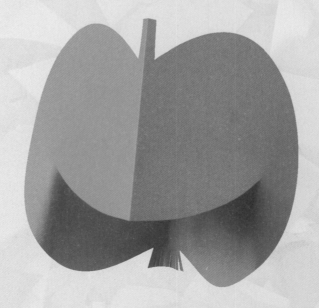

Pear

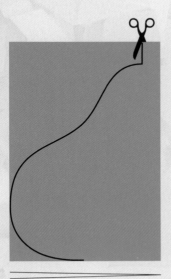

1. Starting at the fold, cut a half pear shape into a folded sheet of size A4 paper. The upper part will be a short stem.

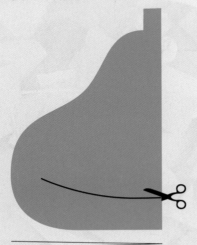

2. Following the picture, make a main cut into the bottom part of the pear.

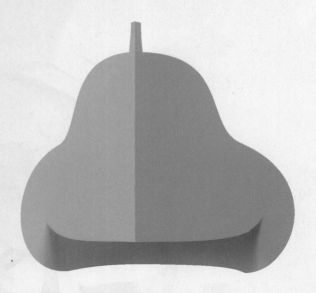

3. Push the bottom part of the mask back and put it on your head.

Lemon

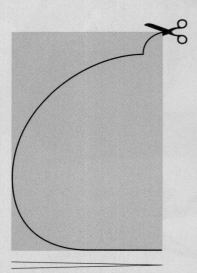

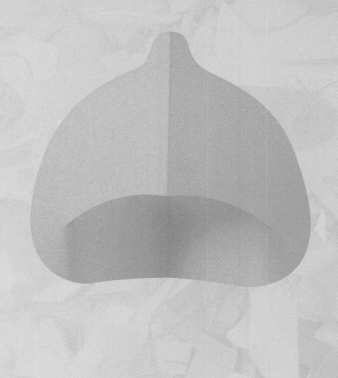

1. Starting at the upper part of the fold cut a small arch into a folded piece of size A4 paper; then continue on and cut a big arch, cutting away the bottom outside corner

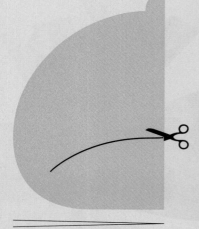

2. Make the main cut in the bottom third of the lemon. Start the cut straight and then start to curve downwards, following the picture.

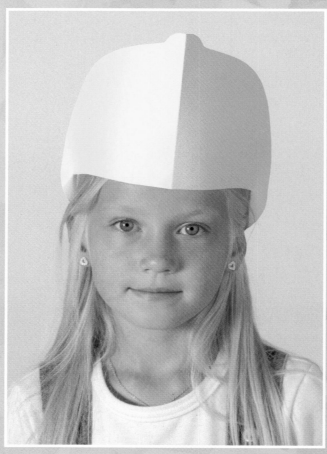

Orange

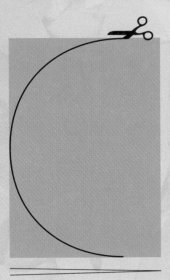

1. Starting at the upper part of the fold, cut a semi-circle into a folded sheet of size A4 paper.

3. Push the bottom part of the mask back and put it on your head.

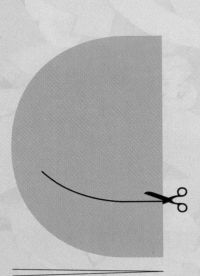

2. Make the main cut to the bottom part of the orange in the shape of a slight curve upwards, following the picture.

43

Daisy

1. Fold a sheet of size A4 paper in half. Starting at the upper part of the fold, cut long slim petals and shorten the petals as you come to the center and then finish with short petals with snubbed edges along the bottom.

2. Make a main cut starting at the middle and angling down and then out, as shown in the picture.

3. Hold the upper part of the mask and pull the bottom back carefully and place it on your head.

Sunflower

3. The sunflower is now ready to wear.

1. Cut the petals in the same fashion as the daisy, but a bit thicker and the cuts should be shorter.

2. Start the main cut a bit higher than half way up and curve it downwards.

Tulip

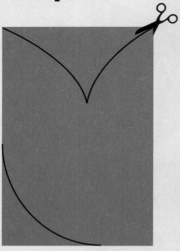

1. Cut a wide but slightly rounded "V" into a folded sheet of size A4 paper. Then, starting near the fold, cut away the bottom corner opposite the fold in the shape of an arch curving upwards.

3. Pull the bottom part back and place the Tulip on your head.

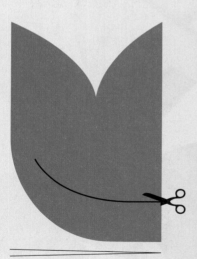

2. Make a main cut perpendicular to the fold, approximately 2" (4 cm) away from the bottom part. It should have the shape of an arch, curving upwards. Finish it approximately 1" (3 cm) from the edge of the paper.

Bluebell

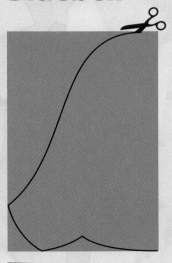

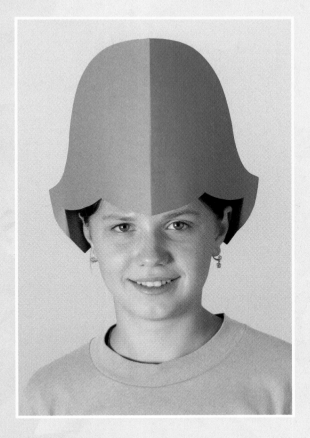

1. Starting at the upper part of the fold and following the picture, cut the shape into a folded sheet of A4 paper. Cut a very wide, shallow "V" into the bottom edge and cut off the corner of the paper with an upward curved cut.

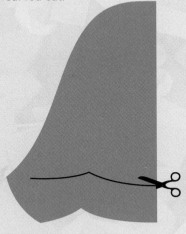

2. Make a main cut to the bottom part of the Bluebell following the shape of the bottom edge.

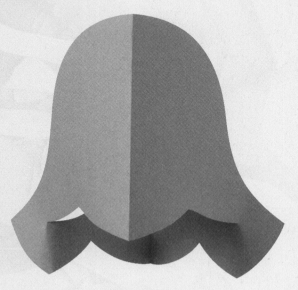

3. Push the bottom part of the mask back and place the Bluebell on your head.

Birdie

1. Starting approximately 1" (3 cm) away from the bottom end of the fold, make a main cut diagonally into a folded sheet of size A4 paper, cutting towards the opposite corner. Finish the cut about 2" (4 cm) away from the corner, following the picture.

2. Following the picture, cut or punch out an eye in the upper part, to the right of the main cut. The eyes do not have to be measured because they are for decoration only.

3. Carefully pull the bottom part of the mask back and the top part forward so that the beak sticks out in front. The eyes will be above your forehead.

Little Frog

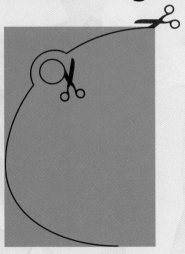

1. Fold a piece of size A4 paper in half. Starting about 2" (4 cm) away from the upper end of the fold, make a curved, downward cut. About mid-way in the cut, make a little arch, into which you will cut or punch out an eye. Make another curved cut, cutting away the bottom left corner.

3. Place the finished mask on your head in the usual way after carefully pulling the bottom part back and the top part forward.

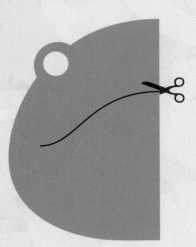

2. Following shape of the top arch, make the main cut about one-third of the way down the fold. Towards the end of the main cut, start to curve it upward slightly.

Kitty

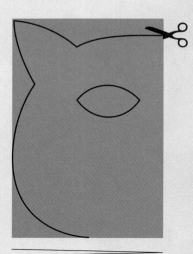

1. Make two wide, shallow V-shaped cuts into a folded sheet of size A4 paper. Start about 1" (3 cm) from the upper right edge and finish in the upper left corner. From the same upper left corner, cut down and around as pictured. Cut out a wide elongated oval eye in the top half of the paper.

2. Starting about one-third from the bottom, the main cut will curve upwards two times. The first smaller curved cut will be the nose; continue with a larger curved cut which will form the cheeks.

3. Pull the bottom part back and the face forward and place it on your head. The eyes will be just above your forehead.

50

Little Mouse

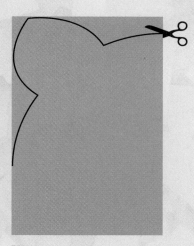

1. Make two slightly rounded, wide V-shaped cuts on the top and left side of a folded sheet of size A4 paper letting the excess paper drop away.

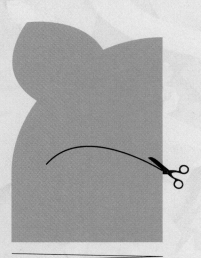

2. In the bottom third of the fold, start your main cut. First it should curve upward and then slightly downwards towards the end.

3. Open the paper and pull the upper part forward and the bottom part back. Now you can place it on your head.

51

Swan

This mask is a bit more complicated. Use a sheet of size A3 paper folded in half lengthwise. You might want to review the descriptions of scoring and bending in the Terms and Symbols section at the beginning of this book. Then you can begin cutting.

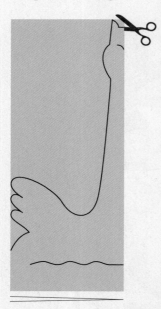

1. Fold your sheet of paper in half lengthwise. Start to cut a half outline of a swan from the upper right hand corner, following the illustration. Start your main cut in the bottom third of the fold; make it a wavy line perpendicular to the bottom of the paper. Cut a little arch where the head meets the beak (for better understanding of the technique for cutting the head and beak, look at the illustrations).

2. Score the paper diagonally on the dotted line.

3. Open the swan and bend its neck backwards to the end at the diagonally scored line.

4. Close the Swan and lay it on its side so that the bent neck faces left. Score the paper diagonally a second time in the upper neck (as shown by the dotted line).

5. Open the neck slightly and fold it diagonally upwards on the new scored lines.

6. Score the sheet diagonally a third time on the dotted line under the head.

7. Bend the neck forward and down on the scored line. Score the beak as marked by the dotted line and...

8. ...open slightly and push the part above the beak inwards.

9. Push the bottom part backwards, place the mask on your head and see if you can gracefully "glide over the surface".

53

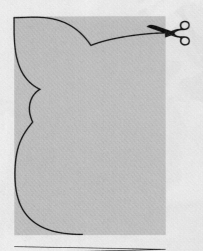
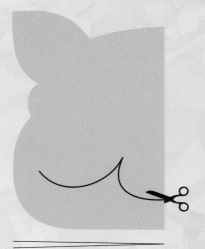
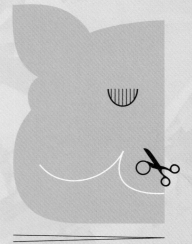

1. Following the illustration, fold a sheet of size A4 paper in half and cut the half shape of piggy's head.

2. Start the main cut perpendicular to the fold; approximately 1" (3 cm) from the bottom edge. Cut the snout with a smaller arched cut and the fat cheeks with a second bigger arched cut.

3. Cut or punch out a small circle in the snout for the nostrils. Make the eyes in the shape of a "U". Make little vertical cuts along the edge of the "U" for eyelashes. When you open the mask, push the eyelashes out and fold them upwards.

Piggy

4. Lastly, you can bend one or both ears down.

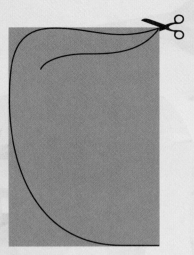
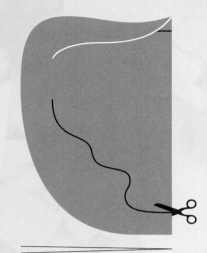
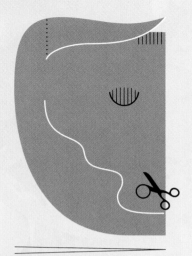

1. Fold a sheet of size A4 paper in half. Start to cut the horns from the upper corner of the fold. Cut a shallow arch along the top edge, almost to the corner. Cut the extra paper away by cutting a large, curving arch to the bottom of the fold. Start a second cut in the same upper corner of the fold as the first cut but make a deeper arch following the same shape as the first cut and ending approximately 1" (3 cm) from the edge. This will form the horns.

2. Make the main cut approximately 1" (3 cm) from the bottom edge of the fold. Starting perpendicular to the fold, cut several wavy lines as shown and end it the same distance from the fold as the cut that formed the horns. Make a small cut from the top of the fold to the beginning of the horns, as shown, and discard the piece.

3. Score along the dotted line. Above the main cut, punch out a circle for the nostrils. Cut out the eyes in the shape of a "U". Make little vertical cuts along the edge of the "U" for eyelashes. Next to the horns, make several small cuts downwards which will form the calf's forelock.

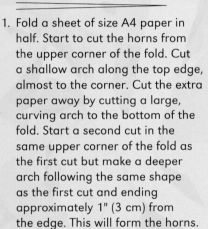

4. Open the mask and bend the horns to the sides. Pull the bottom part of the mask backwards and you can put it on your head.

Calf

55

Bullfighter

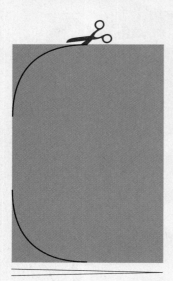

1. Fold a piece of paper in half and with two arched cuts, cut away and discard both corners on the side opposite the fold.

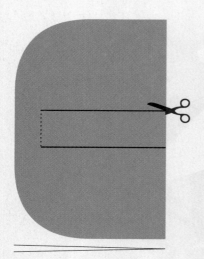

2. Make two perpendicular cuts equidistant from the center of the fold, about 1" (2 cm) from each other. End them approximately 2" (4 cm) from the opposite edge. Score along the dotted line.

3. Open the cap slightly and push the strip out and squeeze. Place on your head with the strip running from forehead along the crown to the back of your head. The wide parts will be above your ears.

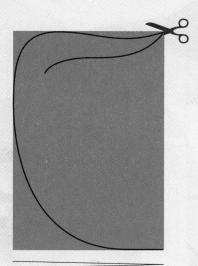
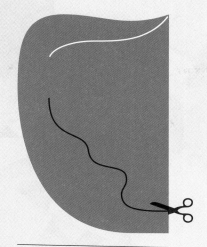
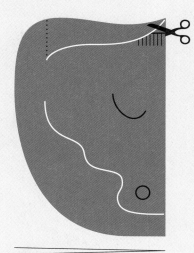

1. Fold a sheet of size A4 paper in half. Start to cut the horns from the upper corner of the fold. Cut a shallow arch along the top edge, almost to the corner. Cut the extra paper away by cutting a large, curving arch to the bottom of the fold. Start a second cut in the same upper corner of the fold as the first cut but make a deeper arch following the same shape as the first cut and ending approximately 1" (3 cm) from the edge. This will form the horns.

2. Make the main cut approximately 1" (3 cm) from the bottom edge of the fold. Starting perpendicular to the fold, cut several wavy lines as shown and end it the same distance from the fold as the cut that formed the horns.

3. Make a small cut next to the horns and discard the piece. Score along the dotted line. Punch out a small circle for the nostrils. Cut the eyes in the shape of a large, backwards "J". Make several small cuts downwards to form the Little Bull's forelock.

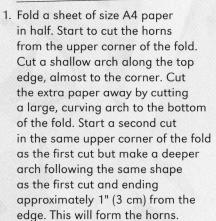

4. Open the mask and bend the horns to the sides. Bend back the eyelids and pull the bottom part of the mask back and you can put in on your head.

Little Bull

The Paper Kingdom wouldn't be a Kingdom without the inhabitants and courtiers. You can cut several masks to represent them.

The King's Royal Court

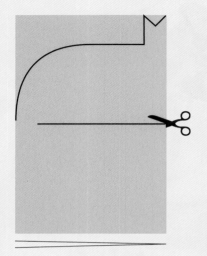 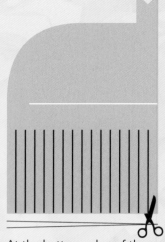 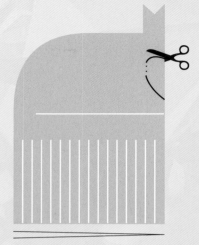

1. Fold a sheet of size A4 paper in half and make a straight main cut about halfway down the fold. Next, cut a crown on the upper right edge of the fold. Continue cutting, following the picture and ending just slightly above the main cut.

2. At the bottom edge of the paper, cut long thin strips about 3" (8 cm) each. These will be the Princess' hair. For curly hair, carefully pull each strip over the edge of your scissors while gently pressing with your thumb. Careful… don't tear the Princess' hair!

3. The mask will be even nicer if you embellish it. To add a little heart to the front, cut a small curved line (like an eyebrow) from the fold. Next, make a lower cut curving upwards towards the first, but do not let them meet. Make sure that the ends of both cuts are equidistant from the fold. Score the area between the cuts.

Princess

4. Open the folded mask and push the paper heart in and squeeze the fold.

A Princess should not only have a crown but also some jewels. Make her a bracelet and a ring.

Bracelet

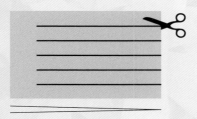

1. Fold a sheet of yellow paper and cut off a strip about 2" (5 cm) long. It should be long enough to circle the wrist, although the ends needn't touch each other. Make four straight cuts from the fold equidistant from each other.

2. Open and thread your hand through the cut strips so that every other strip is on the opposite side of your wrist.

Ring

1. You can make a ring in a similar fashion with the strip you cut away from the bracelet. Fold the long edge of the paper upward about one-third.

2. Make two equidistant cuts from the fold almost to the top of the folded piece. From above, also make two equidistant cuts going downwards towards the edge of the folded piece but not through it.

3. Curl the upper strips with your scissors and thread the Princess' ring onto your finger in the same way as the bracelet.

61

King

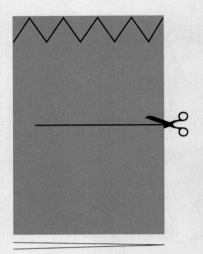

1. Fold a sheet of size A4 paper in half and make a perpendicular main cut approximately in the middle of the fold. Cut a series of small "V"s along the entire top edge creating the points of the Royal Crown.

2. Create a gemstone over the forehead by making two small angled cuts into the fold midway in the top half, one down from the top and one up from the bottom, but do not let them meet. Score along the dotted line.

3. At the bottom edge of the paper, cut long thin strips about 3" (8 cm) each. These will be the King's hair. If you wish to have curly hair, just carefully run each strip over the edge of your scissors while pressing gently with your thumb.

4. Open the folded mask and push the "gemstone" in and squeeze the fold. Pull the bottom part backwards and the upper part forwards and place on your head.

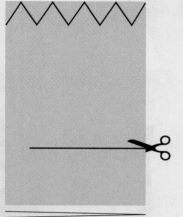

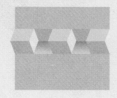

Queen

4. Pushing them alternately inwards and outwards, create little windows. They will represent a row of jewels along the circumference of the crown.

1. Make the main cut into a folded sheet of size A4 paper lower than it was on the King's crown. Cut a series of small "V"s along the entire top edge. Open the sheet of paper...

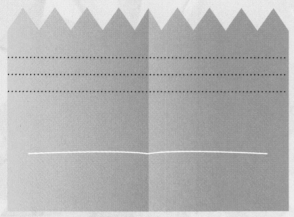

5. Make sharp folds under the ends of the main cut. Pull the bottom part of the mask backwards, place it on your head and you can begin your reign.

2. ... and fold it three times accordion-style parallel to the main cut.

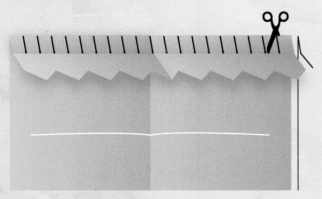

3. Open these folds and then fold down the middle fold. Make perpendicular cuts just to the edges of the accordion folds, approximately ½" (1 cm) apart.

63

Courtier

Proceed in a similar fashion as you did with the Queen's crown but before you fold the paper, curl it slightly by pulling the shorter side over the edge of a table.

1. Shape the main cut following the illustration. Score along the dotted line.

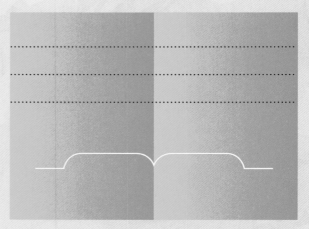

2. Open the sheet and make three accordion folds in the upper part.

3. Open these folds and then fold down from the middle fold. Make dense perpendicular cuts just to the edges of the accordion folds.

4. Straighten the upper part of the mask so that the folded strips are facing forward. Make two folds to pull the bottom part backwards. Place the mask on your head.

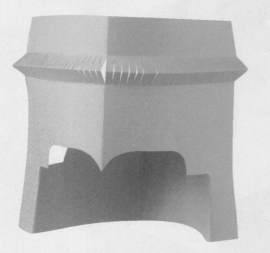

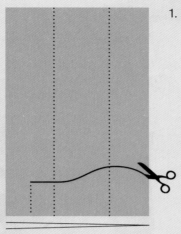

1. Proceed as you did with the Queen's crown, but this time curl the paper by pulling it over the edge of a table. Start the main cut in the lower third of the paper. Begin with an upwards arch and then back down again as shown. Score along the dotted lines.

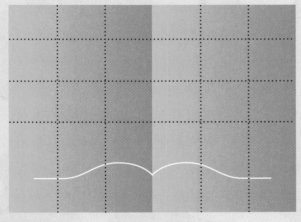

2. Open the sheet and make three accordion style folds in the upper part. They can be wider than in the Queen's crown.

Lady-in-Waiting

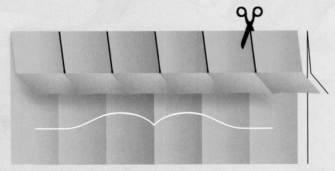

3. Open the folds and then fold down from the middle fold. Make wide perpendicular cuts just to the edges of the accordion folds.

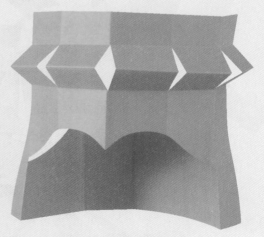

4. Pull the bottom part backwards and the mask can be placed on your head.

65

Knight

For the Knight's mask, use thicker paper approximately 1" (3 cm) wider all around than size A4.

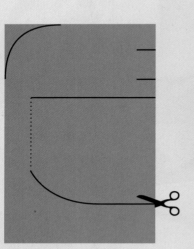

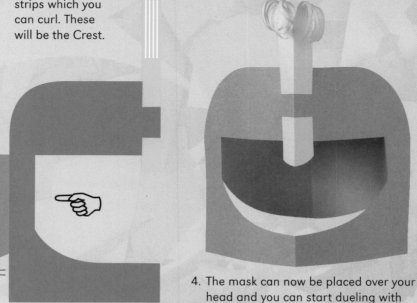

1. Create the Knight with two main cuts, both ending approximately 1" (3 cm) from the opposite edge. The lower cut is arched upwards. Score along the dotted line. Round out the top left corner by cutting an arch, creating the silhouette of the helmet. Make two short perpendicular cuts of the same length from the fold in the top third of your paper and...

2. ...cut a thick strip that can be inserted into this cut. Fold this strip in half lengthwise and cut the upper part into thin strips which you can curl. These will be the Crest.

3. Insert the strip into the cuts so that the bottom comes down to represent a nose protector. Open the mask slightly and push the middle part of the mask inward and squeeze the fold.

4. The mask can now be placed over your head and you can start dueling with a dragon!

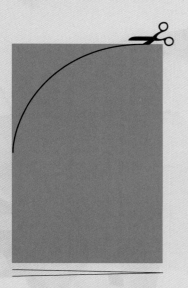
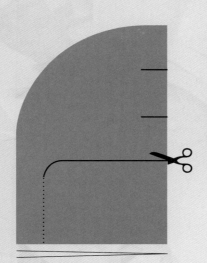

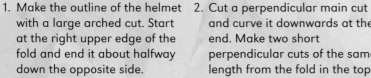

1. Make the outline of the helmet with a large arched cut. Start at the right upper edge of the fold and end it about halfway down the opposite side.

2. Cut a perpendicular main cut and curve it downwards at the end. Make two short perpendicular cuts of the same length from the fold in the top third of your paper and...

3. ...similarly to the knight, insert a lengthwise strip of folded paper of another color. The strip should be longer than the upper part of the mask. Cut the top on a diagonal to create a sharp point, the bottom will be a nose protector.

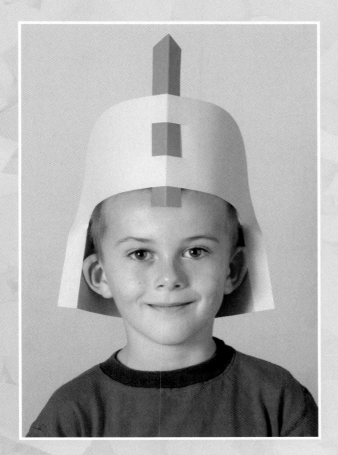

4. Now, place the helmet on your head.

Royal Guard

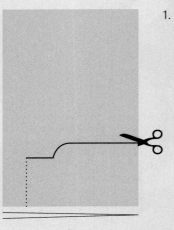

1. Round out a piece of A4 paper as you did with the Courtier's mask and then fold it. Make the main cut in the bottom third. Start it perpendicular, then make a little arch downwards and then straight again to finish about 1" (3 cm) from the left edge.

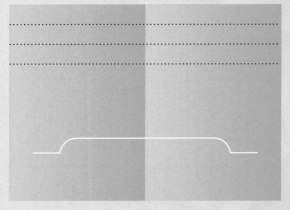

2. Open the sheet and make three accordion folds to the top third of the sheet. Open the folds and then fold down from the middle fold.

Cook

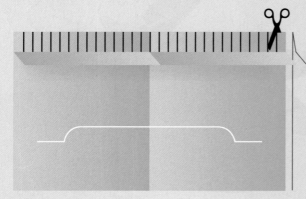

3. Make many thin, short cuts downwards just to the edge of the folds. Open and fold the top third back and down and squeeze the fold.

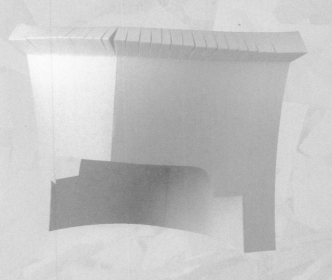

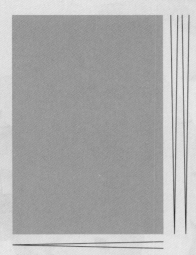

1. Fold a sheet of size A4 paper in half lengthwise and then in half crosswise.Hold the paper so that the side with one fold is on the left and the edge with two folds is on the bottom.

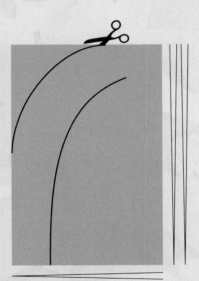

2. Cut off the left upper corner with an arched cut. About 1" (2 cm) from the bottom left edge, start an arched cut towards the right upper corner and finish it 2" (5 cm) from the fold.

3. Open your cap so that the V-shaped gaps are in the back and front and the curved edges are facing down towards the ears.

Nanny

Court Jester

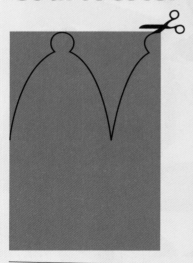

1. A jester usually has a cap with three points that have bells on the points. In order to achieve the three points, you have to cut one and one-half points into the upper edge of a folded sheet of size A4 paper. Holding the fold facing right, start the cut at the top of the fold and continue as illustrated.

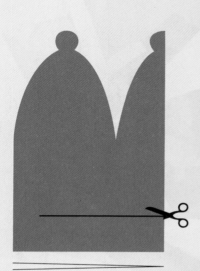

2. Make a straight main cut in the bottom part. You may make the cut in any shape you desire.

3. When you open the mask, you may fold down one point if you wish to.

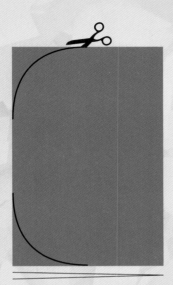

1. Fold a sheet of size A4 paper in half and cut off the top and bottom corners on the edges opposite the fold.

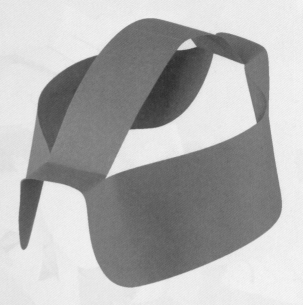

3. Place the cap on your head with the center strip over your head, placed from front to back of the head. The curved edges will face down and the sides will cover your ears.

Hunter

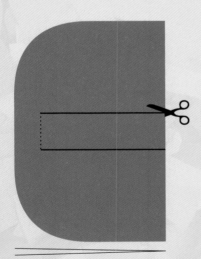

2. Find the center of the fold and make one straight cut on either side of center, approximately 2" (4 cm) apart. Finish the cuts 2" (4 cm) from the opposite edge. Score along the dotted line.

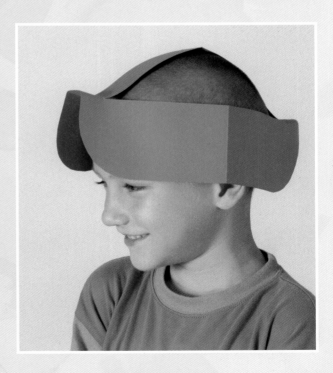

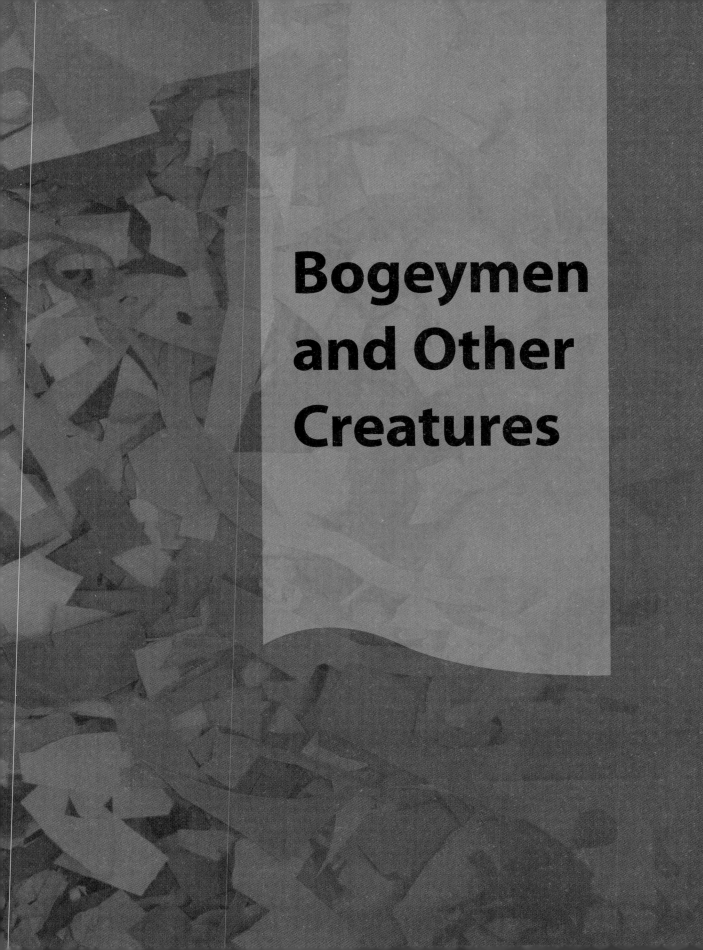

Bogeymen
and Other
Creatures

1. Use a large size sheet of paper (A3) so that the cap will be high enough. Fold it in half lengthwise with the fold to the right. Starting at the top right corner, make a diagonal cut that ends at the bottom third of the opposite edge.

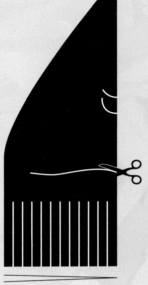

2. Make a wavy main cut and hair as shown in the illustration. About halfway up from the main cut, make two small arched cuts upwards that do not meet. Open the paper, push in and squeeze the fold. This will be a lying down moon ornament in the cap.

3. Open the mask and start performing magic!

Various Bogeymen and other mysterious creatures belong in every proper kingdom and they will not be missing from ours.

Sorcerer

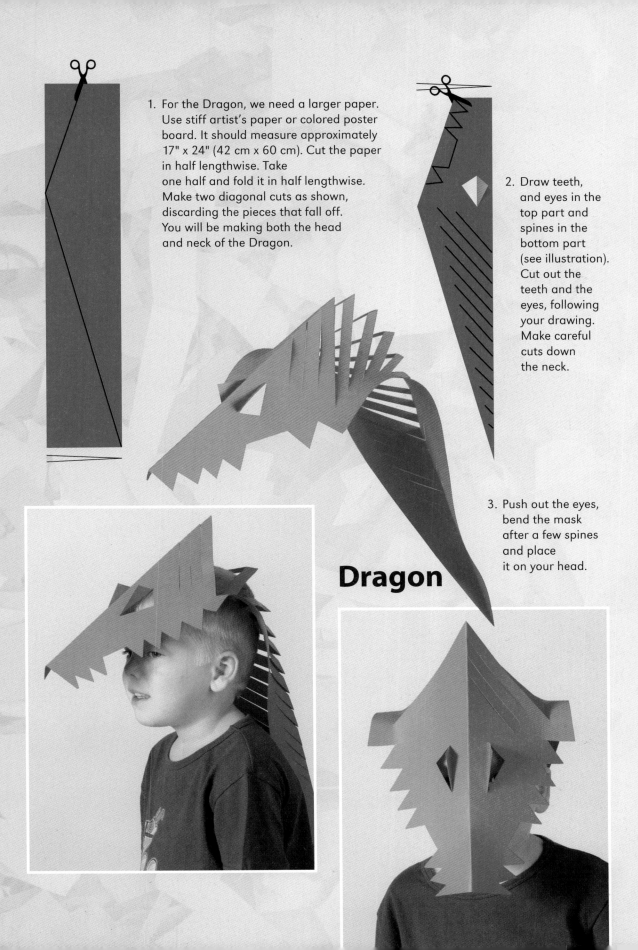

1. For the Dragon, we need a larger paper. Use stiff artist's paper or colored poster board. It should measure approximately 17" x 24" (42 cm x 60 cm). Cut the paper in half lengthwise. Take one half and fold it in half lengthwise. Make two diagonal cuts as shown, discarding the pieces that fall off. You will be making both the head and neck of the Dragon.

2. Draw teeth, and eyes in the top part and spines in the bottom part (see illustration). Cut out the teeth and the eyes, following your drawing. Make careful cuts down the neck.

3. Push out the eyes, bend the mask after a few spines and place it on your head.

Dragon

Skeleton

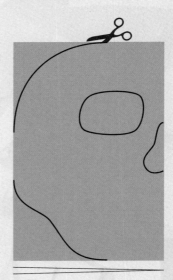

1. Fold a white sheet of size A4 paper in half. Draw an outline of half of a skull with one eye and half a nose, as shown in the picture, and cut them out.

2. Make the main cut into the fold under the nose. Start with wavy lines for the teeth and finish with a long curve upwards.

3. Pull the bottom part of the mask backwards and put it on your head. The upper part of the mask goes above your forehead. The cut-out eyes are not really for looking through.

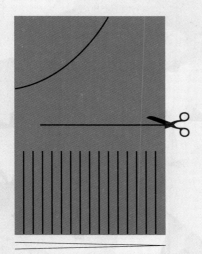

1. This is a very easy mask. Fold a piece of size A4 paper in half. Make a curved cut from the middle of the top to about one third of the edge. It represents a hat. Make a main cut in the middle of the fold. The strips at the bottom will be the long hair. You can curl them softly if you wish.

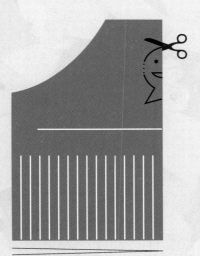

2. Make two cuts into the fold above the main cut to create a fish. Poke out the eyes with the point of your compass and then cut the mouth. Score along the dotted line. Open the paper slightly and push the fish through.

3. Pull the bottom of the mask backwards and place on your head.

Water Sprite

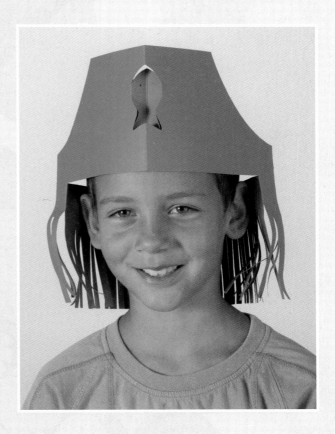

1. Fold a sheet of size A4 paper in half. Cut off the bottom corner opposite the fold with a curved cut upwards. Stick a pointed scissors in the mid-bottom and make two curved cuts. The upper cut should be longer than the bottom cut; when you open the mask you will have "tusks".

2. Make slightly curved cuts about 1" (3 cm) above the tusk and finish about 2" (4 cm) from the opposite edge. When you reach the top, make the last cut another curve and throw away the extra paper. Bend the tusks downward, one from either side.

Sea Monster

3. Open the paper and put it on your head. Pull it down so that the tusks are near the outside corners of your eyes.

Demon

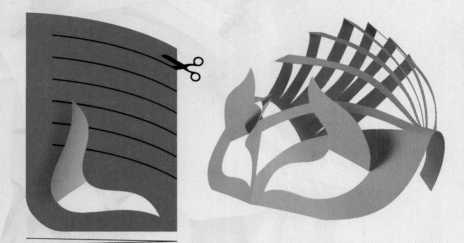

1. Fold a sheet of size A4 paper in half. Cut an arch into the bottom edge opposite the fold. Next make two cuts following the picture. The upper cut will be shorter and the lower one longer. These cuts will be the horns.

2. Make a series of slightly curving cuts about 1" (3 cm) starting just above the top of the horns to the top of the paper. When you reach the top, make the last cut another curve and throw away the extra paper. Bend the horns upward, one from either side.

3. Open the mask and put it on your head. Pull it down so that the horns are near the outside corners of your eyes.

From Ancient Egypt

It seems to me that well known masks are not enough. So, digging deep into history, I found some old friends. These masks represent ancient Egypt.

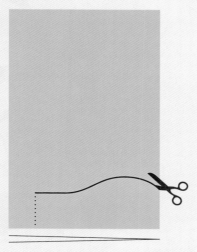

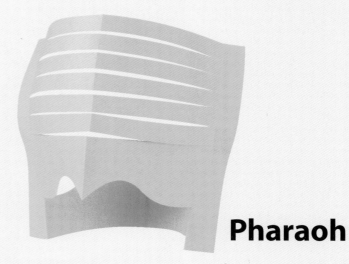

Pharaoh

1. Use a stiff sheet of A4 for this mask. Fold the paper in half with the fold on the right. Start to make a main cut with a slight curve upwards and then down again; finish with a straight cut about 1" (3 cm) from the opposite side. Score along the dotted line.

3. Open the paper. Fold the sides down from the main cut. To make the strips rounded, pull gently over the edge of a table. This mask should be made of stiffer paper so that the side strips will hold the upper part in proper form.

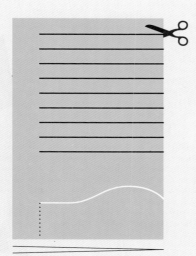

2. About 2" (6 cm) above the main cut start to make horizontal cuts perpendicular to the fold. These cuts should be about 1" (2 cm) appart. They should reach the same distance from the fold as the main cut.

Pyramid

When we hear about Pharaohs, we also think about the pyramids; huge buildings made from heavy stone blocks. So, if you are going to be the Pharaoh, you must convince a friend to be a pyramid!

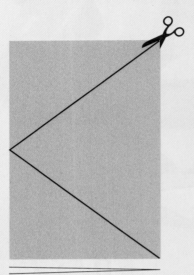

1. Fold a sheet of size A3 paper in half. Cut out a triangle.

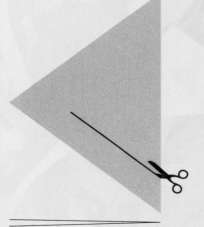

2. Make a main cut parallel to the bottom, about 2" (5 cm) from the edge. Pull the bottom part back and fit it on your head. But remember, you are a pyramid, not a blockhead!

82

Sphinx

The true Sphinx is a huge, lying stone figure with a human face on a lion's body. Of course, our Sphinx will be made of paper.

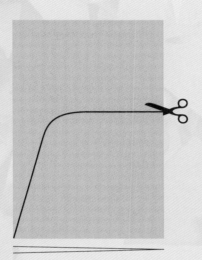

1. Fold a sheet of A3 paper in half. Cut out the same line as in the illustration.

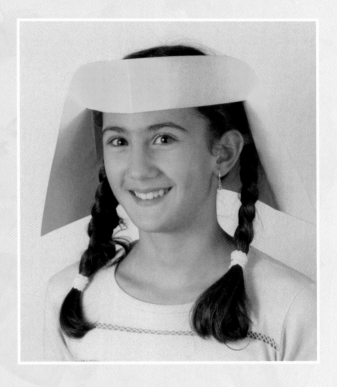

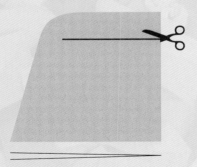

2. Make a main cut about 2" (6 cm) from the upper edge.

3. Push the bottom part of the mask backwards and put it on your head.

Creatures from Outer Space

While I was showing the inhabitants of the Paper Kingdom how different masks are made, I remembered a modern fairytale about interplanetary adventures, visitors from outer space! At once, I made up my mind that extraterrestrial masks must not be missing from the Carnival. I taught citizens of the Paper Kingdom how to make them and I will teach you as well.

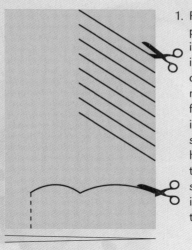

1. Fold a sheet of size A4 paper in half. Round it slightly by pulling it gently over the edge of a table. Make the main cut about 2" (5 cm) from the bottom and in the shape of one full shallow arch and one half arch. Score along the dotted line. Cut seven diagonal strips into the fold, following the picture.

2. Let the last diagonal cut go all the way to the top edge and discard the extra paper. Push the bottom part backward.

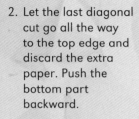

Girl Extraterrestrial

3. Open the mask. Bend the first strip upwards from both ends. Do the same with the third, the fifth and the seventh, following the picture.

4. You will have a nice criss-crossed diamond form above the forehead when you place the mask on your head.

Boy Extraterrestrial

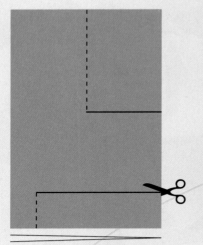 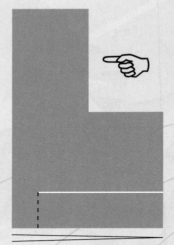 

1. Fold a sheet of size A4 paper in half. Make a straight, perpendicular main cut from the fold about 2" (5 cm) from the bottom edge. Finish the cut about 2" (5 cm) from the left edge. Make a second cut from the fold about halfway and end it in the middle of the paper. Score on the dotted lines.

2. Push the upper part inside as far as the edge of the cut. Squeeze the new folds so that they will be parallel to the main fold.

3. Now, push the same part back and cut strips from the main fold as you see in the picture. Finish the cuts about 1" (3 cm) from the new fold. Before you cut, draw lines with a ruler so that the strips will all be the same size.

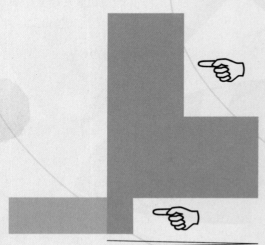 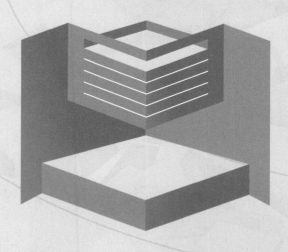

4. Push the whole upper part inside. Push the bottom part under the main cut backwards and pull it to the other side. Squeeze the folds.

5. Open every other strip slightly and then push them forward. Shut the mask and squeeze the folds.

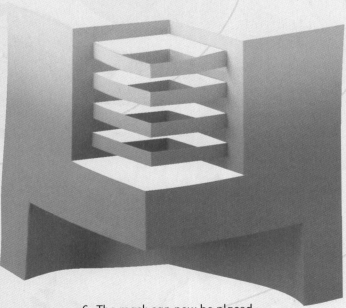

6. The mask can now be placed
on your head.

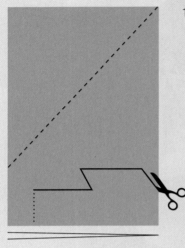

1. Fold a sheet of size A4 paper in half and then fold both halves diagonally as shown by the dashed line. Start a main cut from the fold. First make a short diagonal cut upwards, then a horizontal one, and then another diagonal cut downwards parallel to the first one. Finish with a straight cut to approximately 1" (3 cm) from the opposite edge. Score along the dotted line.

2. Make four parallel cuts into the upper part of the mask, perpendicular to the diagonal fold. The two cuts in the middle should be longer and the two outside ones should be shorter. Score along the dotted lines.

Martian

3. Open the upper triangle pieces and push the strips inside, pull them to the end of the cuts and squeeze the folds.

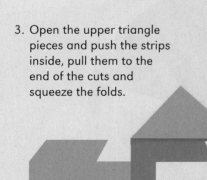

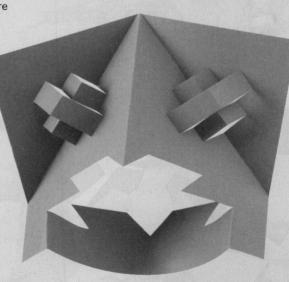

4. Open the upper triangle slightly as you see in the picture. Pull the bottom part below the main cut backwards and put on your Martian mask.

Venutian

1. Make a vertical fold in a size A4 sheet of paper. Make ten equidistant diagonal cuts of about 1" (3 cm) each. Start the first cut just above the right bottom edge, going upwards at about a 45 degree angle. Finish each cut about 2" (4 cm) from the left edge of the paper.

2. From a distance of approximately 1" (3 cm), fold up the bottom left corners so that they are parallel to the first diagonal cut. From this triangle, make two straight 1" (3 cm) cuts, one vertical from the bottom edge and the other horizontal from the left edge.

4. Bend the mask into an arch, and open the triangles before you place it on your head.

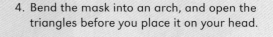

3. Open slightly and push the paper from these short cuts outside and squeeze the folds.

Princess' Toys

and Nets for Dragon

These were the masks which I taught the inhabitants of the Paper Kingdom to cut. And, I hope, you also!

By the way, we had to find a solution for a serious problem. During the Carnival, the wings of Dragon Shredder fluttered above the castle again. I had to do something so that he did not frighten Princess Notepad and the entire Kingdom when I leave. I told them that they must always have fairytale books with them and when Shredder appears they must begin to read. If they are deep into a story, no paper dragon will see them. But they objected. We can't always be carrying fairytales, they said. So, I advised King Notebook I to have the clouds full of paper nets so that if Shredder appears, he will get wrapped up in the nets.

Net

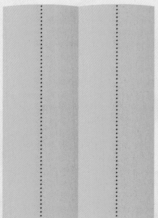

1. Divide a sheet of size A4 paper in four equal parts...

2. ...which means you should fold it in half and then in half once more...

3. ...so that you wind up with a thin strip.

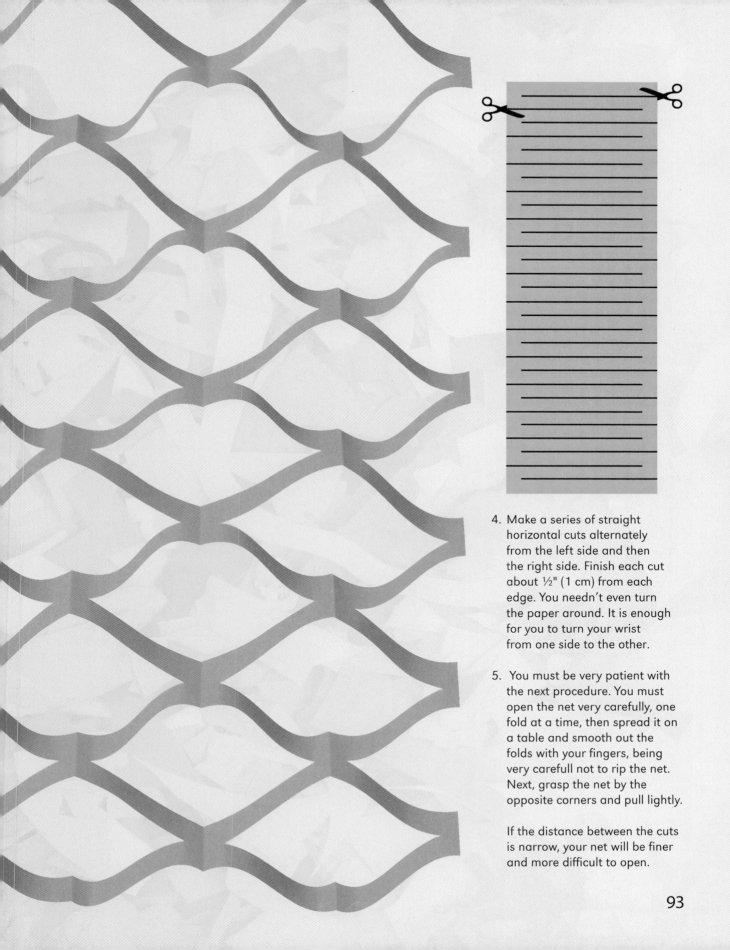

4. Make a series of straight horizontal cuts alternately from the left side and then the right side. Finish each cut about ½" (1 cm) from each edge. You needn't even turn the paper around. It is enough for you to turn your wrist from one side to the other.

5. You must be very patient with the next procedure. You must open the net very carefully, one fold at a time, then spread it on a table and smooth out the folds with your fingers, being very carefull not to rip the net. Next, grasp the net by the opposite corners and pull lightly.

If the distance between the cuts is narrow, your net will be finer and more difficult to open.

If Dragon Shredder should try to sneak up on the castle by land, I told the inhabitants of the Paper Kingdom to hang this Bell Net above the castle gate.

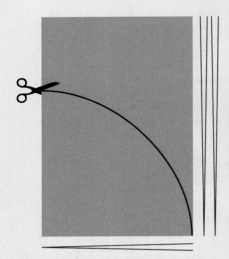

Bell Net

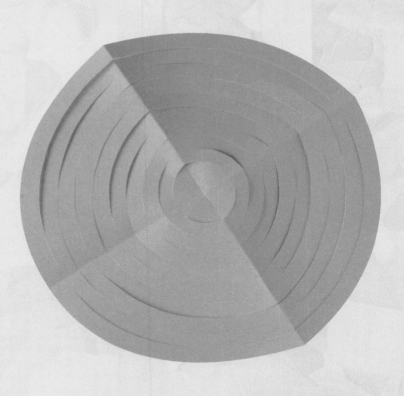

1. Fold a sheet of size A4 paper in half and then in half again so that one fold faces left and the second fold is at the bottom. Grasp the bottom left corner and make a curved cut from the right bottom corner midway up to the left edge, creating a quarter-circle.

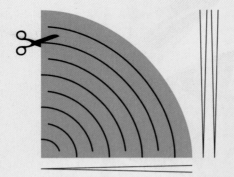

2. Make similar curved cuts parallel to the curved edge, first from one side and then from the other. Each cut should approach the opposite edge but leave a piece of paper intact there. Continue in this fashion to the bottom left corner.

3. Unfold the paper carefully, smoothing the folds as you go.

4. Pull a thread through the center at the very top of the net. Pull the thread up and the edges down and your net will unfold in the shape of a bell.

Dainty Bell Net

Use the thinnest paper you have for the dainty bell net.

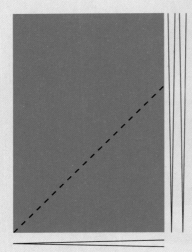
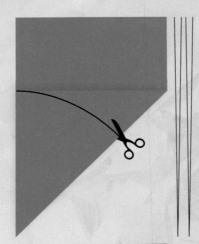

1. This is made in a similar fashion as the last but, when your paper is folded in quarters, bring the bottom right corner up in half once more.

2. Cut a curved line from one edge to the other, as shown in the illustration. Discard the cut away top.

3. Make alternating curved cuts from one edge almost to the other, leaving a bit of paper intact at the end of each cut.

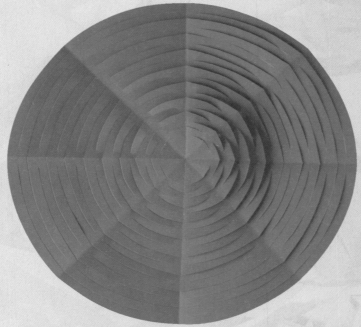

4. Unfold carefully, smoothing the folds as you open each one.

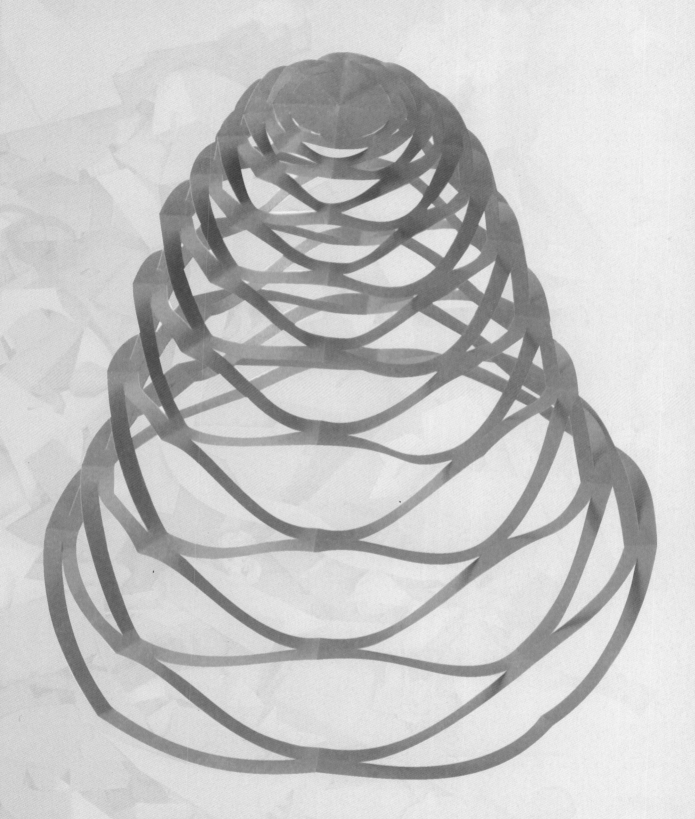

5. Pull a thread through the center. Pull the net up, stretch it out, and you are
   ready to help catch Dragon Shredder.

We hung the clouds and the main gate with paper nets so that the inhabitants of the Paper Kingdom and Princess Notepad could quietly sleep or play. What kind of toys does she have? Well, paper ones of course! Her toys are like many others: they open their mouths, blink, wave their wings and even peck. The only difference between these toys and others is that these can be made by anyone.

Chick

1. For this little chick you only need a quarter of a piece of size A5 yellow paper, folded in half. Since this chick was just hatched from its egg, it will be like an egg with one small difference: it will have wings on its sides. So, cut out a half-egg with a wing as shown in the illustration. Make a short perpendicular cut in the upper side of the fold, about the same level as the wing. Use your hole punch to make an eye above it. Score along the dotted lines.

2. Open slightly and, from the back, push the top part of the beak in and up and squeeze the fold. Do the same with the bottom, pushing downwards.

3. Now you have created a little beak. Hold each wing and as you slowly open and close, your chick will "peep".

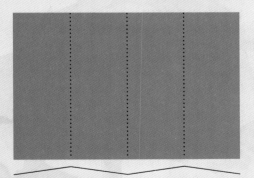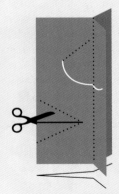

1. Fold a sheet of size A5 paper in half vertically and then open it. Turn it over and fold each half in half again. Turn it again and fold along the original fold so that all four quarter are accordion stacked.

2. Hold the folds to the right and make an arched cut upwards in the upper half. Score along the dotted line.

3. Make a straight cut in the bottom third of the middle fold, perpendicular to the bottom edge. This cut should be longer than half the width of the folded parts.

4. Open the paper slightly and push the top eyelids in and up and squeeze along the creases formed the by the scored lines.

Sleeper

5. Open and hold the paper on the edges between the eyes and mouth and slowly pull open and closed. Your Sleeper will yawn and blink his eyes!

Singer

1. Fold a quarter of a sheet of size A4 paper in half. Cut out a half-circle with an ear on the side. Cut out a little circle for the eyes in the upper part with either a hole punch or a manicure scissors. Make three curved cuts to create a mouth in the bottom part. Make the middle cut longer, the upper and lower ones shorter. Shape the top cut to represent a lip.

2. Open the paper and push the cut parts of the paper inside. Pull the upper lip and curve it upwards. Curve the bottom lip downwards and then squeeze the folds in order to create sharp folds.

3. Hold your singer's ears with both hands. Open and close the paper and the singer will open and close his mouth. Help him sing by lending him your voice!

100

1. Fold a sheet of size A5 paper in half lengthwise. Following the picture, draw a butterfly, and then cut it out. First cut out its head with feelers, the big front wings and the small part of the little bottom wings. Next, curve the cut to the left and slightly upwards so that you cut away the extra paper around the butterfly. Lastly, from the fold, cut out the end of the body and the front part of the bottom wings. Score along the dotted line.

Butterfly and Tulip

3. Hold the edges of the paper between the butterfly and tulip. Open and close the sheet gently and the butterfly will flutter its wings. You can also color and hang the paper on your wall for a beautiful picture.

2. Make two cuts into the fold in the bottom part of the sheet to create a tulip. Score along the dotted line. Push the butterfly down and inside, push the tulip inside, and fold along the scored lines.

Woodpecker

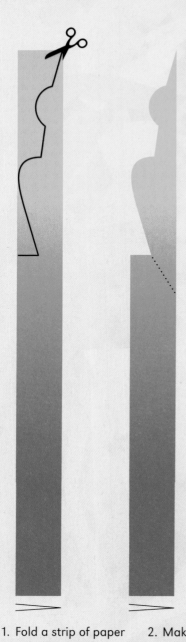

1. Fold a strip of paper in half lengthways. Cut a half-outline of a woodpecker. Start your cut at the top right end of the fold for the beak, then the head, long neck and body with closed wings.

2. Make a straight cut from the left side of the paper to the wing and discard the extra paper. Score the paper diagonally downwards (see illustration).

3. Where the scoring meets the fold, open the paper. Push the woodpecker inside out and squeeze the folds along the scored line.

4. Unfold the paper. Below the woodpecker, fold the paper up. This will place the tree in front of the woodpecker. The woodpecker will be in a slanted but almost vertical position against the tree. Squeeze the folds carefully as shown.

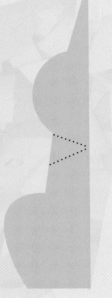

5. Score along the dotted line on the woodpecker's neck and fold the head upwards, so the beak will stand up. With your thumb and forefinger, hold the woodpecker under the head...

6. ...and with the finger of your other hand, open the head and push it forward.

7. When the head is in the right position, press the fold.

8. Hold the side edges, where the woodpecker's body ends. Pull it gently in and out and the woodpecker will peck the tree.

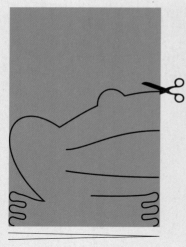

1. Fold a sheet of size A5 paper in half and draw half the outline of a frog. Start to cut with slight curve downwards from the fold. This will be the top of the head, cut out a bulging eye and then cut downwards to the back leg and toes. Start the frog's mouth about one fourth of the distance from the top of the frog's head and make a slight cut curved downwards. The mouth cuts should go almost to the frog's leg. Make the same sized cut a little lower and slightly curving upwards. Cut the frog's other toes from the right fold.

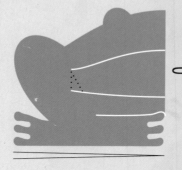

2. The ends of both cuts must be the same distance from the fold so they will open vertically and diagonally along the score line. Score vertically from the end of one cut to the other and then diagonally from the top cut, going right just a bit to meet the bottom cut. Fold along the scored lines.

Frog

3. Open the frog slightly and hold the sheet between the two cuts and push it in and down so that it folds along the scored lines. Squeeze the folds. When you hold the frog by the edges and pull it open and shut, the bottom part of the mouth will move to croak.

Greeting Cards

Princess Notepad often sends greeting cards to her friends who live in the Paper Kingdom. Because she is very skillful and really loves her friends, so she usually makes and decorates the cards herself. Wouldn't you like to make somebody happy by sending a card you've made yourself? Follow the directions in the next few pages for beautiful holiday cards.

Note:
For cut greeting cards, do not fold your paper in half. Just fold it over one-third from the left and you will have plenty of room for a message on the right hand side. After your message is written, fold the other third over the first and it should fit easily into an envelope.

Small Window Card

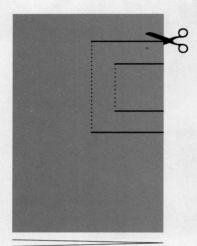 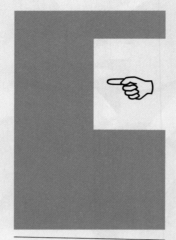 

1. Fold a sheet of paper in half. Starting at the fold, make two perpendicular cuts of the same length into the top half of the paper. Make another two longer cuts a short distance on either outer side of the shorter cuts. Score the paper on the dotted lines.

2. Push the paper between the longer cuts to the other side and squeeze the folds.

3. Push the paper between the short cuts back. Squeeze the folds.

Heart Card

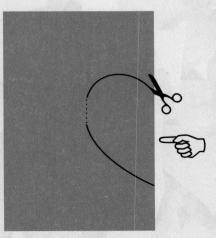 

1. Make two curved cuts as shown into the fold. Both ends should reach the same point. Score along the dotted line.

2. Open the card and push the heart inside. Squeeze the folds. When somebody opens the card, they will know you send your love.

Easter card

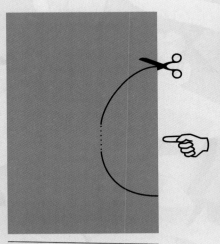 

1. Make an outline of one-half an egg. Both ends should reach the same point. Score along the dotted line.

2. Push the egg inside. Squeeze the folds. Color your Easter Egg as you wish.

Christmas Card

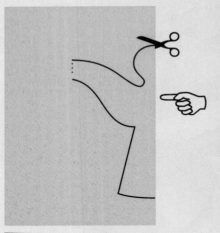 

1. Make two cuts to create an outline of one-half of an Angel. Both cut ends should reach the same distance from the fold. Score along the dotted line.

2. Push the little angel inside. Squeeze the folds.

Winter Card

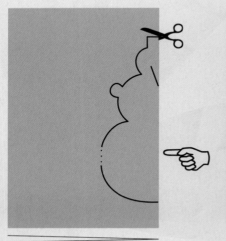 

1. Following the illustration, make two cuts to create the outline of one-half of a Snowman. The top cut will form the snowman's hat, head and middle snow ball with hands. The bottom cut will curve upward and will form the bottom of the biggest snowball. Both cut ends should reach the same point. Score along the dotted line.

2. Make a small, sharp diagonal cut into the top snowball to create a nose. After pushing the snowman to the other side and squeezing the fold, fold back the top of the diagonal cut to form the nose.

New Year Card

1. Fold a sheet of paper in half and lightly draw the outlines of Christmas trees with a pencil. Start your cut from the top right of the fold, following the picture, and end at the bottom left with a rounded edge.

2. Next draw an outline of a little house. Make two cuts. The first begins just above the halfway point of the fold and curves downwards with a small curve inwards at the bottom. The second cut begins near the bottom, goes perpendicular and curves up at the end. Both cuts should end at the same point. Score along the dotted line.

3. The third cut begins a little bit above the first cut and is again in the form of a Christmas tree. The edge will meet the edge of the first cut. Discard the extra paper.

4. Make two short perpendicular cuts with curved ends in the little house, one up and one down. Score on the dotted lines.

5. Open the paper slightly and push the house forward into the card. Squeeze the folds. Now you can send your joyful wishes for a Happy New Year to your closest friends.

On the Tail End

I did not fly away from the Paper Kingdom by helicopter, but decided to go back through the tunnel. If I had flown out by helicopter, I would have felt dizzy. I originally entered the Paper Kingdom by creeping through a large paper box but, for some reason, nobody believes me. The box was taken away by somebody and now I can't return to the Kingdom.

Why, you ask, do I want to go back to the Paper Kingdom? Well, I forgot to take the 1,999 drawing papers which were given to me by King Exercise Book I.

Well, never mind! I have plenty of sheets of paper here. I have enough to cut out the entire Paper Kingdom according to my memories and I am sure that now you, too, can cut something out as well.

Yours, Karol Krčmár

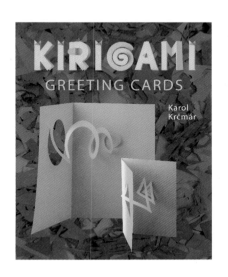

KIRIGAMI
GREETING CARDS

Karol
Krčmár

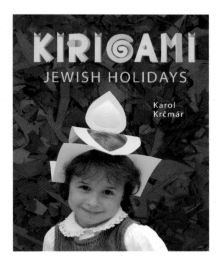

KIRIGAMI
JEWISH HOLIDAYS

Karol
Krčmár

Until we meet again in my other Kirigami craft books

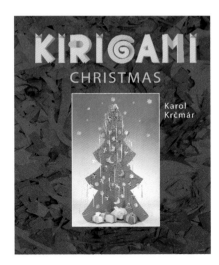

KIRIGAMI
CHRISTMAS

Karol
Krčmár

Karol Krčmár

KIRIGAMI
THE PAPER KINGDOM

The Art of Paper Cutting and Folding

Typography: Radoslav Tokoš
Graphic design: Karol Krčmár and Radoslav Tokoš
Photos: Jiří Hološka
Editor: RNDr. Jela Šimeková
Translation: Mgr. Štefan Patrik Kováč
Published by McCabe Children's Press
A division of Kotzig Publishing, Inc.
Printed in Slovakia
112 pages, 1st edition

www.kotzigpublishing.com

ISBN 0-9715411-6-7